ONE COUPLE'S GIFT

or

WHAT TO DO WITH THE FAMILY FORTUNE AFTER YOU HAVE EARNED IT

featuring

Harold and Louise Nielsen,
the
Foldcraft Corporation, an ESOP,
the
Winds of Peace Foundation,
and the
Third World Friends Store,
both NPOs.

Steve Swanson
Steve Sheppard
and others

Nine Ten Press
910 St. Olaf Avenue
Northfield, MN 55057

Nine Ten Press
910 St. Olaf Avenue
Northfield, MN 55057

ISBN 0-9657762-1-2

Cover, illustrations, and interior design
Judy Swanson

Editor
Shelley Swanson Sateren

Printed by
Engage Print, Inc.
1000 5th Street West
Northfield, MN 55057

CONTENTS

1

HOW IT ALL BEGAN

About 20 years ago, the late Paul Newman mixed up a batch of salad dressing in his basement laundry tub, bottled it, and gave it to his friends as gifts. The product caught on. Employees were hired. A business evolved. Teamed up with his old friend, author A.E. Hotchner, Newman has since plowed $150 million in profits into thousands of charitable organizations.

The title of the book that Newman, his wife, Joanne Woodward, and Hotchner released said it all: *Shameless Exploitation in Pursuit of the Common Good.* Newman added:

> There is a tremendous amount that the business community in this country can do to counter the very bad image of America that has been occurring with Enron ... and unilateral war. ... They should take the challenge and run with it. (*Newsweek,* 11/3/03, 48–49)

The little book you hold in your hand raises that challenge. It is addressed to business leaders, entrepreneurs, inheritees, and other people of some means. The effort doesn't have to be massive. The people *Time* magazine named as persons of the year for 2006 (January 2) are doing the Newman thing in a gigantic way.

Microsoft's Bill and Melinda Gates have teamed up with rock singer Bono to lobby government and to fund programs for improving world health that will channel efforts worth billions.

Reading about massive efforts, we might ask, "But what can *I* do?" This book will address that question by looking at the life, work, and vision of one man and one woman, and what they have done with their more than modest success in founding and building a company in southeastern Minnesota called Foldcraft.

I began hearing about Foldcraft Corporation when I was pastor of the Dennison-Vang Lutheran parish 10 miles east of where we now live, about 40 miles south of Minneapolis—Northfield, Minnesota, the home of Carleton and St. Olaf colleges.

Like many two-point parishes, Dennison-Vang had a split personality. The Dennison Congregation was Northfield-Minneapolis oriented and the Vang church did their schooling, shopping, and health care in Kenyon and at Mayo-famous Rochester. My parish hospital calls were often over 100 miles apart.

Kenyon, in southeastern Minnesota, is a land-locked farm town of 1,661 [city limits sign] people, many of them Scandinavian, mostly Norwegian. Foldcraft is its major industry.

Members of my Vang church—*many* of them—worked at Foldcraft, a company that back then I knew only by name. They were cabinet makers, welders, spray painters, technicians, and assemblers who, I later learned, helped to manufacture furniture for shopping malls and fast food restaurants like Dairy Queen, Subway, and Hardees. Later, to show they don't boycott corporations on the other end of the employee benevolence spectrum, they have been shipping furniture also to Walmart for their employee lunchrooms.

I never visited Foldcraft during the three years (1975–78) I was pastor in the area and only vaguely knew where, exactly, in Kenyon that manufacturing complex stood.

But a curious set of circumstances made me more and more aware of Foldcraft. Having unilaterally, perhaps foolishly, cut myself loose from a secure and tenured college professorship in Canada in 1974, I soon—and later—discovered that U.S. college faculties had suddenly gotten serious about racial diversity, gender equality, and youth. Being a middle-aged male of English and Scandinavian stock meant that for the next 25 years I would never again teach full time. So to feed our family I preached, taught, and worked with my hands—often at three or more half-time jobs. We began, between preaching and teaching assignments, buying old houses and fixing them up for rent or sale.

Among my home buyers in those years was a pleasant young engaged couple named Robin and Renee. Being a full-service real estate dabbler, I not only sold them a house but officiated at their wedding and later baptized their first child.

Robin's last name was Nielsen. I began hearing about his late father, Richard, who left his work as an educator to become national sales manager of his brother's business. The brothers worked together in this corporation I had heard about years earlier—Foldcraft in Kenyon.

Robin hadn't, back then, fully gotten over his father's untimely death. He wondered out loud if Richard, his late father, had worked *too hard* for brother Harold.

That was my introduction to Harold Nielsen, owner and founder of Foldcraft, Inc., Kenyon, Minnesota.

My other source of Nielsen information was also coincidental and offhand. A writing student.

My 30 years of half-time teaching at my alma mater, St. Olaf College, in Northfield, Minnesota, was in writing. In graduate school I was trained to teach modern English and American Literature and writing—but writing was my specialty and first love—and fortunately, what St. Olaf needed.

In January of 1978, an adult student named Steve Sheppard appeared in my creative writing class. A 1971 graduate of Luther College, Decorah, Iowa, Steve, I later learned, was on a four-year leave of absence from Foldcraft. He wanted to write a novel.

Steve soon showed himself to be a fine writer, a dedicated student, and a valuable and articulate member of a writing section otherwise made up of twenty year olds.

Steve and I became good friends that year. We had a lot in common beyond our first names and our mutual love of writing. We were both products of Lutheran colleges; we belonged to the same Northfield congregation; we had both adopted Korean kids —and a few years later, we became around-the-corner neighbors.

Again Foldcraft and Harold Nielsen popped up in conversations. I began to hear not only about a company that used to employ a lot of my former parishioners, but a company that had some very high-minded attitudes toward its employees and business practices—attitudes that later rolled over into philanthropy.

It seemed unlikely that this high-minded company could have worked brother Richard to an early grave.

My writing student, Steve Sheppard, after working as Human Resources Director there for 15 years, was promoted to CEO of Foldcraft when Harold Nielsen began a long, phased, retirement process. The company introduced an Employee Stock Ownership Plan (ESOP) to prepare for that time, and the corporation was gradually sold to its employees.

A major portion of Foldcraft's sale price became the underpinning for The Winds of Peace Foundation, a philanthropic organization that was founded and organized by Harold and Louise Nielsen initially to fund a children's home in Mexico. Winds of Peace gradually evolved into a broad spectrum humanitarian agency that worked in Belarus, Mexico, and Central America—mainly Nicaragua.

The more I learned about Harold and Louise Nielsen, the more interested I became. Several times over several years I asked my friend and neighbor, Steve Sheppard, "Should I be thinking about writing Harold Nielsen's story?"

"I'll ask," Steve said.

Reports always came back from Kenyon that Harold didn't want to make any fuss over himself or what he was doing—that he didn't want to toot his own horn.

I had never met Harold Nielsen.

Finally, on June 29, 2002, I found myself officiating at a 30th anniversary wedding vow renewal for Steve and Katie Sheppard. The extended family turned out for this event, including Steve's dad and mom. I learned that Richard Sheppard, Steve's dad, had been, before retirement, a vice president at 3M Corporation. A gracious, stately, and articulate man, he looked very much like the CEO type that he was—and I began to understand where Steve got the stuff to run a company. Our mutual experience with service-oriented church colleges reminded me also why Steve gravitated toward a company like Foldcraft and a mentor like Harold.

Also attending the ceremony that evening, sitting in a front pew with his wife, was an older man who looked a lot less like a CEO. He looked more like one of my Vang parish farmers—the kind of guy who may have owned land, buildings, and machinery worth a couple million dollars, but one you would never pick out of a crowd as being wealthy.

[More than one insurance agent or other Foldcraft visitor with a portfolio to sell has rued the moments he brushed off as unimportant, maybe a janitor or something, the soft-spoken guy in suspenders—later to learn that he owned the company.]

At the reception later, I met this man, Harold Nielsen, and his wife, Louise. We got to talking. I said at last, "I've wanted to write your story."

"That's what I heard," he responded.

"What do you think?" I asked.

"I'm not much for making a fuss," he said.

For the next five minutes I outlined my approach. "I wouldn't be so much writing about you," I said, "except for how you got from where you were to where you are now."

"OK," he said.

"And about the responsibility of wealth," I went on, "even small amounts of wealth," I said. "Not necessarily millions," I said, "but tens of thousands. Wealth like many Americans have."

Harold just smiled.

This is not the story of a businessman who built up a company from nothing to quite something. Thousands of American entrepreneurs have done that. I wouldn't bother to write about any of them.

This is a story of one of those successful businessmen who woke up late in the voyage, beginning at last to see the world a bit more like his wife had seen it all along, and then saying to himself, "I'm going to make my business success mean something."

One of Minnesota's most famous novelists, Ole Rolvaag, was one of my father's teachers. His kids, Ella and Minnesota Governor Karl, were regular speakers in my writing classes. Ole Rolvaag, along with composer F. Melius Christiansen, helped put our little St. Olaf College on the map.

But, more important than any of this, in all his writing, and in his interaction with the Lutheran Church, and in the ever expanding Norwegian immigrant community, Ole Rolvaag was a moralist. Like Harold and Louise Nielsen, Rolvaag struggled in his writing and in his life, to understand the human cost of industrial development, capitalism, and the westward movement. It was an enigma to him, a moral quagmire. Here's what he said:

Neither Yankee nor immigrant has been able to determine the proper relationship between earning money and using it in the interest of human well-being.
(*Ole Rolvaag,* Jorgenson and Solum, p. 100)

Many successful business people have shared this concern. In 2007, for instance, Peter G. Peterson, sold Blackstone Group, a firm he co-founded, and became an instant billionaire. Like Harold, he asked himself, "What to do with so much money?" His challenge, he writes in *Newsweek* (3/7/08, 56) is our epidemic of national selfishness and the national debt we are leaving our young people. He concludes his article by quoting one of my personal heroes, the German martyr-pastor, Dietrich Bonhoeffer,

"The ultimate test of a moral society is the kind
of world it leaves to its children."

Harold's *Christmas Carol*-like epiphany is what this story is about: a humble couple who achieved the American Dream but then were forced to back away from the rewards of a lifetime of material earnings and business achievement, and to face up to Ole Rolvaag's mysterious relationship between earning and philanthropy.

Harold and Louise have had to muster up the courage to look at where capitalism had gotten them, to compare that to where they *wanted* to be in "retirement," and then to begin deciding what to do next.

2

HAROLD

Harold Nielsen was born in 1916, the first of six children—four boys and then two girls. This was not a huge family for the early decades of the 20th century, but it became a challenge for his mother, Marie, when, in the spring of 1937, Harold's father was injured and two days later died after falling from a building construction scaffold. He was setting stone for the new telephone building in downtown St. Paul, Minnesota.

His widow Marie and her six children got a whopping $80 a month for a little over seven years until his worker's compensation ran out. Then they were on their own.

Marie did not remarry for almost 20 years. When she did, it was to a grade-school friend from Denmark who had never married. She raised the children herself—and of course they also were encouraged—indeed forced—to become self sufficient.

I'm guessing there was a certain Danish immigrant stubbornness in Marie's determination to raise her family alone through those mid- and late depression years. Her own family history contributed to that decision. Her father had died back in Denmark when she was ten—leaving her to become the family dairy maid. When her mother died in 1910, she emigrated alone to the United States and began working as a housekeeper in Iowa. She was 21.

She thrived on hard work. She must have, since she lived to be 104. Her story is chronicled in a biography called *Marie,* by Vivian Elaine Johnson (Family Narratives, 1990, 129 pp.).

Marie's work ethic and determination were transfused into her family. For starters, all four of her boys, *all four brothers,* became Eagle Scouts. That was quite a record in scouting—four Eagles in one family.

It's not that easy to become an Eagle Scout. It's like a youthful liberal arts education in the great outdoors and requires some wisdom, resourcefulness, and above all, tenacity. I was about two-thirds there when I gave up.

Decades after being in his troop, Harold established a memorial to their scoutmaster, Mr. Kingsbury. He named a 24-unit senior citizens low-income housing project KINGSBURY COURT.

A second project also has a memorializing name in keeping with Harold's world-view. He called it LINDER-WILLSON VILLA, a 12-unit, low-income housing complex named after Linder, an activist American engineer who was martyred, assassinated, while trying to construct a small dam to electrify a rural hospital in Nicaragua, and Willson, also an activist, who lost both legs under a train while protesting at a nuclear pollution site in California.

Both structures are in Kenyon, Minnesota, and sit on land owned by Harold and Louise. Both are subsidized by the Farmers' Home Administration.

The land on which these housing complexes were built was trackage from a bankrupt railroad company which Harold had bought on speculation. Such land transactions are built into the Nielsen family entrepreneurship that blossomed early. Among the first enterprises the family founded was a pair of made-on-site ice cream parlors in residential neighborhoods in St. Paul. These stores were a learning experience until World War II began.

Suddenly sugar was rationed and ice cream became a pre-war luxury. The businesses were turned over to an employee and all four of the boys joined the military. Oldest brother Harold spent the next forty months as a radioman in the Merchant Marine.

Following the war, Harold gravitated toward woodworking—cabinet making and millwork production. The early woodworking years and also some of his personal attitudes were outlined for me over lunch at Little Oscar's Restaurant at Hampton near Hastings, Minnesota. There I met Sam Hertogs, himself a writer and a long-time friend and legal counsel of Harold's.

Around 1948, according to Sam, Harold set up shop in Mendota, an old Mississippi River town south of St. Paul. For $20 a month, he rented his first building, an 8 by 66 foot, dirt-floor cowshed built on a hillside. His first owned building was half cement floor, half dirt. On the dirt side they dug a latrine, which had to be shared with their one female employee, until Harold could afford to install plumbing.

He called his business Nielsen Millwork and Manufacturing Company. While in Mendota through the 1950s, Harold bought a lot of property, much of it with title problems (hence his need for Sam's advice). "Mendota was a wild town," said Sam.

In 1961 Harold moved the operation to Faribault, back then on U.S. 65, now on I-35, about 50 miles south of the Twin Cities. This was a litigious period for Harold and his business—and looking back, those hard-nosed employer-employee relations in Faribault stood in sharp contrast to who he has become and how his Kenyon business operates today.

For instance, Sam said Harold successfully (which is to say he won) defended himself in court and waited out a strike by the Teamsters' Union who tried to organize his shop.

The union retaliated by turning OSHA loose on him, resulting in citations for 50–60 violations. Again Harold fought it out and had to accept responsibility for only one violation.

Sam told of several other ventures—a business in Mendota called Minnesota Quartz Company, owned by his former cow-shed landlord. When the landlord died, Harold bought the company. He bought other properties and other businesses. Some questionable partners also surfaced. Certain ventures worked out beautifully, others didn't.

While all these other ventures were coming and going, the little furniture factory he had started, Foldcraft, Inc., was growing, diversifying, and getting ready for its final move. In 1967, Foldcraft moved from Faribault to Kenyon (more of this later).

One of the Mendota millwork ventures piqued my interest especially. Among the most popular prints sold during the 1950s by Augsburg Publishing House in Minneapolis, the literary/theological resource center of my church, was a picture of this saintly looking old man with his hands folded, praying over a loaf of bread and a bowl of soup. It was called "Grace." I had seen it in dozens of dining rooms in both the U.S. and Canada. Harold told me the man pictured was a depression era hobo who, in exchange for food, had sat for his portrait in the photographer's kitchen.

Harold bought, from Augsburg, at 40 cents each, 40,000 16x20 inch copies of this print, framed them in black walnut, then turned around and sold them for $4.21 each to Curt Carlson's Gold Bond Company to be used as a premium, redeemed by books of Gold Bond trading stamps. That's how they got from his Faribault and Kenyon shops to so many of my neighbors' and parishioners' dining rooms.

Speaking of parishioners, Harold has had his moments with the church. For one thing, it moves too slowly for him. For another, he's never too sure the church has its priorities in order. Harold is, for instance, remembered at First Lutheran Church in

Kenyon for speaking out at a congregational meeting against repairing the leaking roof over the church when, as he pointed out, children in Central America had no roof at all over their heads.

Bruce Kjellberg, an old friend of ours, was Harold's pastor back at that time. He was interviewed for a 1983 Religion Section article about Harold in the Minneapolis *Star-Tribune*. Kjellberg called him—and Harold agreed that he had often been—a "burr under the saddle" of the church. Kjellberg explained that to me in a letter 15 years later:

> "His methods and outspokenness rankled people but I think it was because he made us all feel ashamed and guilty."

Kjellberg went on to say that because of this, Harold wasn't always treated kindly in Kenyon. He was, for instance, chosen "Citizen of the Year" in 1990 by the Kenyon Lions' Club, an honor muted somewhat by some of Kenyon's finest boycotting the banquet.

Several years later, the title was broadened from town to county. In 1993 Harold was named "Goodhue County Citizen of the Year." No one boycotted.

Kjellberg went on to write that:

> "In my 40 years of ministry, Harold would probably rank as the church member I knew as the most committed to causes of social justice and world hunger."

Perhaps knowing and respecting Pastor Bruce Kjellberg was inducement enough for Harold to accept an assignment representing Kenyon's First Lutheran Church at a World

Hunger Conference at St. Olaf College in the mid 1970s. The speaker was George Johnson, who represented what was then The American Lutheran Church. Johnson was also Kjellberg's brother-in-law. Perhaps in sending Harold to this seminar, there was some hopeful pastoral manipulation.

That conference, and Johnson's inspiring presentation, exploded into a lifetime of involvement for Harold and Louise. It started with an introduction to Joel Mugge, then Director of the Center for Global Education at Augsburg College in Minneapolis. That led to travel—and an awakening—that Harold himself once called a "conversion."

Here is the experience, in Harold's own words, excerpted from a talk he gave at historic Holden Lutheran Church, rural Kenyon, on Good Friday, April 21, 2000:

> "In August, 1983, Louise and I went on an experiential learning trip conducted by the Center for Global Education at Augsburg College. We spent two weeks in Mexico, Honduras, and Nicaragua. On the second day, in Cuernavaca, Mexico, we visited the worst slum I had ever seen—filth, terrible housing, no roads, bridges, or infrastructure. Nothing.
>
> "As I stood looking at this mess, something encircled one of my legs. There at my knee was a little fellow, about 2 years old, naked as a jaybird, his arms wrapped around my leg, hug fashion, and looking up at me with a big friendly smile. He ran off then, and was out of my life forever— but has been in my thoughts ever since.

"That was my introduction to the global community.

After seeing, for the first time, such abject poverty, Harold woke up at 3 a.m. the next morning in Cuernavaca, Mexico, weeping. "You don't have to go to the university," he said afterward, "to see something is wrong."

> "He hadn't cried in years," columnist Kari Larson wrote, describing Harold's experience in *Business Ethics,* "then memories of four years in the World War II merchant marines flooded back: death and destruction in the Philippines, Australia, North Africa, and developed European countries … and Antwerp, when a black service man's dead body lay exposed for days, floating in the harbor, while white corpses were immediately shrouded and set aside. I asked why, and the white officer in charge replied, 'Oh, it's just a nigger.' I had repressed all that so I could come back to the U.S. and be a part of the same system." (March/April, 1995, p. 35)

In a novel called *Q* (Harcourt, 2004, 170), set in Reformation Germany (1517–55) the preacher narrator says:

> "Have you ever wondered how much time an Antwerp merchant spends accumulating his fortune? Simple: His whole life. His whole life to accumulate it, to fill his safes, his strongboxes, to build a prison for himself and his own male offspring, and dowries for the females. … I want

to persuade them that a life free of enslavement
to money and commodities is a better life."

Harold's epiphany was of the same sort that many of us watched in the film *About Schmidt*. After a lifetime of working for Woodman Insurance—and after suddenly losing his wife—Schmidt became aware that something was wrong. He asked himself, "Has anything I've ever done in my whole life had any value?"

Harold may not have asked himself that question, but after a successful business career he had a similar experience. Harold and Louise responded, and it changed their lives.

The epiphany that Louise Nielsen had been quietly engineering for years, Harold finally experienced in the 1980s. It has since benefited hundreds, indeed, thousands of people, people with different kinds of needs in Kenyon, southern Minnesota, Mexico, Belarus, Nicaragua, and elsewhere in Central America.

Harold didn't become a dishrag. He didn't just weep for the poor of the world. Rather, like the reformed Ebenezer Scrooge, who also had been moved by poverty and suffering, Harold became an advocate for the poor, the underprivileged, the dispossessed—and later through micro-financing helped empower the under-challenged and under-funded budding entrepreneurs of Nicaragua. Harold helped people who just needed a start. Like the real life industrialist Schindler, who wept for not having done enough, for not having saved more Jews, Harold and Louise are doing what they can, while they can.

David Harris of Red Wing, Minnesota, a medical doctor with extensive ties to Nicaragua, writes this about Harold:

He is attentive to others, listens carefully, and then speaks out without haste but with an underlying passion and fearlessness, and sometimes a penetrating little dig, that refuses to accept the status quo. Harold is a quiet revolutionary— a wolf in sheep's clothing. He sees through the system with a clear-eyed understanding of the human cost and a vision of justice that demands a better response to human suffering.

3

LOUISE

You'd have to look a long time to find a woman as quietly gracious as Louise Nielsen. "How can two people that old," writes John R. Tobin of Minnesota South Central Technical College, "have so much energy and charm?"

You'd think, talking to Louise casually, that she'd never had a nickel's worth of turmoil in her entire life. You'd also wonder as I have, looking at her, if she was in pain from the disappearing cartilege in her spine. She is not in pain, she says, though the condition does look painful, and slows her down a bit.

Historically, however, Louise has had to negotiate a few bumps in her life—especially early on. She was born in 1915 in St. Paul to middle class parents. Her father, a successful insurance man kept an office on the 16th floor of the downtown St. Paul Pioneer Building. Louise's first office job, right out of high school, was in her father's office.

She describes him as a hot-tempered man, but very loving. Louise and her only sister [who died at age 40] were never punished corporally, and only verbally on occasion.

The family moved from their St. Paul neighborhood to White Bear Lake, today a teeming Twin Cities suburb, but back then a cozy lakeside town. She graduated from White Bear High School in 1933, having specialized in shorthand and typing.

A gregarious young woman, Louise married Harold Peters in 1941, "too young," she later pleaded. After giving birth to a daughter, Rosalind, and two sons, Marvin and Stephen, in her first four years of marriage, and after suffering through some of her husband's failed enterprises, she once threw a coffee pot at him. "When anger takes over," she said recently, "your brain doesn't work."

Her father finally intervened and took her away from her get-rich-quick, ne'er-do-well husband. "I never harbored any hard feelings toward my first husband," Louise said quietly. "He just never settled down." Her marriage had lasted four years, right through World War II.

Her father ensconced Louise and her young family in the downstairs of a duplex he bought especially for her and his grandchildren. Her husband left for California and disappeared from their lives until years later when he resurfaced in Sacramento, California, three months before his death. When his sons, Marvin and Steve, learned he was dying, they brought him home to White Bear Lake to die quietly.

Louise's father was able to support her through the children's infancy. Louise went back to work when Rosalind was seven and old enough to enjoy being left with her grandma. The boys were content to spend time in daycare ($4.50/week for the two of them).

Her first working-mother job was with Farwell, Ozmun, Kirk, a hardware company. She then took a job with 3M, only a few blocks from where she lived. At 3M she soon worked her way up to $200 a month, a massive wage for a single mother in the late 1940s. In her rent-free situation it was a fortune.

The young woman who lived upstairs in their duplex felt sorry for Louise, home alone all the time, and invited her along on Sunday night expeditions to the Prom Ballroom in St. Paul.

Minnesotans my age and older remember the Prom, not from being there, but from their Sunday night Big Band live broadcasts on Minneapolis radio. We high school kids listened regularly, 40 miles south in mid-century Northfield, sometimes danced to the music on the paved Carleton College tennis courts. There at the Prom Ballroom, on one of those Sunday nights, Louise met Harold.

On that very first night, as he was driving her home after the dance, he proposed to her. She laughed and said no. After going with her for two more years he finally asked her again. This time she said yes.

Some time after their marriage she suggested they have a fourth child together. This time Harold said no. Three is quite enough, he said.

As you can imagine, their marriage prompted family trepidation on both sides. Louise's parents, after her earlier marital fiasco, urged caution. Harold's mother, Marie, wondered out loud about a romance with a divorcee who had three kids.

"Did you have trouble with Marie?" I asked Louise in a recent interview.

"Not at all," she said. "Once things were settled, she treated me like a daughter—sometimes even *better* than her own family."

"Pastor Kjellberg told me she lived with you later on," I interjected.

"Yes. Her last years were with us. We couldn't have gotten along better."

Louise and Harold started dating during the hopeful, glorious, and booming post-war recovery period. He didn't whisper sweet nothings in her ear when they danced—he whispered statistics. "He was an encyclopedia of statistics back then," she said. "He still is."

She soon learned Harold was an entrepreneurial wheeler-dealer. One of their early dates was spent transporting and carrying down into her mother's basement 40 typewriters that Harold had purchased for a song and hoped to re-sell for a symphony. "He did sell most of them, as I remember," Louise said, smiling.

Another of their early dates consisted of *her* doing *his* books. She became, not long after their marriage, his business account-ant. She learned cost accounting, sales, office, and advertising skills by being very attentive to professionals who visited their office and by asking them a lot of technical questions. Of course anyone to whom 3M paid $200 a month back then also had to be very bright and very capable.

Harold and Louise were married in 1950, a prosperous time in U.S. economic history, and a wonderful era for both matrimonial and opportunistic business starts.

Harold early on adopted Louise's three children and loved and cared for them as his own—insofar as a busy businessman could. Their oldest, daughter Rosalind, and later one of Rosalind's children, Laura, became accomplished artists. Their older son, Marvin, lives in New Jersey and produces educational documentaries for film and TV. He has created several films for Harold and has contributed to the TV series *Captain Kangaroo*. Their younger son, Stephen, is a self-employed woodworker. All three, it seems, are creative.

On a recent visit to my house to exchange ideas about our concurrent biographical projects, Sylvia Conger, Rosalind's daughter (Harold and Louise's granddaughter), spotted a still-life oil painting of a pair of gourds, framed and hanging prominently in our dining room.

"That looks like one of my mother's paintings," she said, pointing.

"Could it be?" my wife wondered. "It's not signed."

Sylvia leaned over the piano and looked more closely. Then they lifted it off the wall and studied it under a light. Sure enough, there, almost hidden in the lower right foreground, was the name: *Rosalind Bonsett*.

Adopted daughter Rosalind must have occasioned some head scratching on Harold's part. After a couple of years at Minneapolis School of Art, she persuaded her mother, Louise, and adoptive father, Harold, to let her continue her art studies in Italy.

"I came home after being abroad," she wrote me in a recent letter, "with a decidedly liberal slant."

Harold, who was, as she noted, a baptized and confirmed Republican at the time, must have blanched when Ros "became involved in Sen. George McGovern's run for the presidency."

Louise was a liberal Democrat and Harold a conservative Republican, bordering, as he puts it, on being a "John Bircher." He later told me with a shrug, "Almost all businessmen are Republicans. Why wouldn't we be?"

Harold and Louise's political differences simmered for a decade until the Vietnam war, then they heated up, "almost to separate bedrooms," Louise said, smiling about it 30 years later.

To indicate how much his views have changed, note his responses to a great-granddaughter's interview paper from April 2003. Erika Davidson was a junior in high school at the time and asked Grandpa Harold many questions about politics and war. Back when it was raging, Harold Nielsen had supported the war in Vietnam. Thirty years later he sang a different tune. Here are his words as Erika quoted him in her paper:

> "[The Vietnam War] showed the vicissitudes of our industrial military complex, and how multi-national corporations exploit the political bureaucracy of our federal government ... at the expense of 50,000 American soldiers' lives and

1 million Vietnamese and innocent women and children's lives. Just like today in Iraq," he added, "the military is the willing handmaiden to the multi-national corporations of the U.S."

One early influence that had to have rubbed off on Harold in the late 1960s was Louise's trip to Mexico with an artist friend. "We spent the whole month of March," she said, "traveling and interacting with the local people. There, for the first time in my life, I saw hopeless poverty—and was deeply affected. I came home and tried to convey the experience to Harold, but it didn't take."

Or did it? Her cold shoulder during Vietnam, her daughter's political rebellion, her anguish over the poverty she had seen—who can say how, in subtle ways, this may have affected Harold? Seeing those he so deeply loved and admired becoming passionate about and concerned for political, military, and social misadventure must have affected him deeply.

Who knows what internal pressures were working in Harold in that decade before his 1983 epiphany? Louise wanted to do something. Harold didn't. Their relationship and attitudes evolved. Challenges presented themselves. A future of service began to weave itself through their lives.

Louise began in small ways, but in retirement, became deeply involved. She organized and with several other women ran "The Gallery," a for-profit wall decor and gift shop. That led in 1989 to the non-profit Third World Friends Store, just a block down the street, now a thriving outlet for used household goods, books, and clothing. (See Chapters 6 and 9.)

Certainly Louise's influence on Harold cannot be underestimated. They have emerged together, are now of one mind, and have been a powerhouse team for good.

Hendrika Umbanhowar, a member of the Winds of Peace Foundation Advisory Committee, puts it this way:

> The Nielsens are not showy, certainly not of the country club set. They understand "establishment," and can move and live in it, but they most certainly do not buy into its myths. The excesses of the marketplace are unpalatable to them. They are pragmatic and focused, down-to-earth realists, with not a shred of hype. They live what they profess. Their actions exceed their words. There is work to be done and they do it. Where others might be discouraged, Harold and Louise are optimistic and hopeful. Their transformed lives have transformed other lives —sharing without end.

4

THE FOLDCRAFT/PLYMOLD COMPANY

Harold's company, Foldcraft, has a steadily growing outreach that expands from its regional and international commitment, not only into issues of global peace, equality, and justice, but also to employee health and welfare.

The Foldcraft plant seems to me to be a fairly large operation. The buildings (275,000 square feet) and grounds (10 acres) cover several square blocks on the southeast edge of Kenyon's residential district. The company employs about 250. Some of them live in Kenyon, some in nearby towns or on area farms. This is also true of Foldcraft's subsidiaries, W.B. Powell Company in Corona, California, and BKR Designs, Inc., and Burgett's, Inc., both in Bloomington, Minnesota.

One of the musts in preparing this volume was to tour, at least once, the Foldcraft plant in full operation. It was easy to arrange. I called my friend and former student, Steve Sheppard.

"I need to tour your plant," I said.

"Have you taken a job with OSHA?" he asked. I could hear the smile in his voice.

"No, I'm still a writer."

"That's even more risky," he responded.

We agreed on a date and time. When I arrived for my mid-morning appointment, a big sign on the receptionist's counter said:

WELCOME
TO
FOLDCRAFT CO.
STEVE SWANSON

The receptionist handed me a form that all visitors are asked to fill out, then called the other Steve down from upstairs. When we had finished our tour and Steve was escorting me back to the reception area, I noticed the receptionist showing a personnel officer my sign-in sheet. They were pointing at me and smiling.

"What's so funny?" I asked.

"We're laughing at what you wrote in the blank where it asks what firm you represent."

She showed the sheet to Steve.

FIRM_____

My entry: "Fairly [firm] for my age, though I'm a bit flabby around the waist."

Touring the plant was an education in itself. We must have walked a mile, back and forth, from area to area—from team to team, I learned later. Some areas were dominated by huge machines. We watched as workers laid in thin veneer sheets coated with heat-activated adhesive. A heated lid came down over these layers of coated wood and pressed them together. Out came a Plymold [the product brand name] contoured seat, which was then cut and trimmed automatically by another machine.

In other areas we watched employees put foam pads and Naugahyde covers over booth benches, fastening them with air-operated staplers.

In the next area, bentwood restaurant chairs were being assembled. Nearby they were being sanded, then wheeled into a spray booth for finishing.

Further on we watched tubular metal chairs materialize through various stages of being cut, bent, and welded together.

When the metal chairs were fully assembled and ready for paint, Steve took me to a station where they were being hooked to a huge conveyor chain that went up overhead and out of sight.

"By the time those chairs reach the other end of that conveyor chain," Steve said, "they will have been washed and dried in five stages, then powder-coat painted, and baked dry. After the padded wooden seats are fastened on, they'll be ready to pack and ship."

"That's a massive conveyor," I said

"I wanted you to see it," Steve said, smiling. "It's an example of how Harold Nielsen thinks and works. About 20 years ago he bought that entire system in California, sight unseen, for $50,000. We had no immediate use for it back then, until a building was built to house it. We sent one of our maintenance personnel to California to supervise taking it apart, hauled it cross country on four 40-foot semis, and then put it back together here in Kenyon after the building to house it was finished.

"They probably called it 'Nielsen's Folly' back then, but look at it now," he went on. "It saves countless work hours, keeps our employees away from sprays and vapors, and has been up and running for several years since we first cranked it up."

"Was $50,000 a good price?" I asked.

"A really good deal," Steve answered.

"Maybe that's why Foldcraft can contribute so generously to charity," I said.

"That's one of the reasons."

Like the Malt-O-Meal cereal company and Carleton College in my hometown, Northfield, Foldcraft is a good place to work —but it's not a place for everyone. Foldcraft emphasizes personal accountability and ownership in its members, as employees are called, in order to maximize the ESOP nature of the Company, and those characteristics are not always easy ones to find in today's labor pool. A 20-year navy veteran who settled in Minnesota tried for several years to land a job at Foldcraft before he finally succeeded. In an interview after a Foldcraft-sponsored Cross Boundaries trip to Mexico, he said this about his reasons for wanting that job:

> "I wanted to work at Foldcraft because I had heard that management treated workers with a lot of respect, and workers treated each other like family—a place where people really care about each other."

The Human Resources staff at Foldcraft work hard to find members like this, people who will take seriously the Employee Stock Ownership Plan (ESOP). Once employed and on the job, they will need to buy into the idea that they are part owners of the company and will be held personally accountable for holding up their end of that interactive bargain.

This partnership mentality has manifested itself in some very different and creative innovations over the years, dating back even pre-ESOP. For example, Foldcraft Company established what might have been one of the very first Employee Assistance Programs (EAP) back in the late 1970s. Recognizing the impact of personal issues on people's ability to function well at work, Foldcraft approached an existing chemical dependency treatment facility with the idea of contracting for counseling services. While the organization had never experienced such a collaboration, it took the risk in providing counseling time, on whatever issues people might bring forth, on a regular basis at the Foldcraft facility. EAP services eventually became commonplace in U.S. businesses, and the service is still available to Foldcraft members.

Foldcraft also pioneered another health-related initiative. The company developed one of the very first health insurance risk-rating contribution plans in the U.S. This pioneering was confirmed by its being cited in *Time* magazine as among the very first plans of its type. The approach essentially put members in charge of their own health practices and costs by relating healthy lifestyles to company contributions for health insurance. Annually, medical personnel visited the Foldcraft facility to conduct assessments of members on health factors that were at least partially under the control of the individual, such as body fat, blood pressure, use of tobacco, etc. Members were never penalized for a condition as long as they had been in medical consultation over it.

Both of these early initiatives stemmed from the company's belief that wellness programming assists members to achieve optimum health, thus reducing their own and the company's healthcare costs. In addition, these programs were felt to create a workforce that would be more reliable, consistent and content with their workplace. Similar innovations were developed that studied improved plant safety.

While touring the plant with Steve, I imagined how a new recruit would be impressed, as I was, at its size, its cleanliness, its logical and labor-saving floor plan and materials availability, and the combination of busy and pleasant people who work there.

From what I knew of employer-employee relationships, it was both fun and surprising to watch the interaction between Foldcraft workers and CEO Steve Sheppard who walked with me. Every interaction took place with a first-name familiarity. After they had exchanged pleasantries or a wisecrack, the members would answer succinctly any questions he or I asked, and then return to work.

The entire company is made up of teams, whether in the offices or the production plant. Within each of these teams, there is a clear effort to communicate to the employee-owners information about the company's performances as well as each unit's contribution on an hour-by-hour basis. It's an instant feedback to members that allows them to take whatever measures might be necessary to meet promises to customers. This is each member's direct "line of sight" to his/her impact on the profitability of the operation. Data such as this drives self-responsibility.

The communication is so immediate and obvious that even a visitor can tell how things are going within a unit. If, in a given one-hour period, the unit under-produces (or under-quotes or otherwise falls short of planned objectives), the numbers on the white board are red and the source of the problem is also noted in red on the board. If the unit is meeting goals, the numbers are in blue. If the team is exceeding its objectives, the numbers are in green.

The value of this feedback system is obvious. Employee-owners who are working for their own success have almost instantaneous data about what they need to do to succeed. Further, if equipment failure or the need to train new personnel results in the unit falling behind goals on a given day, members recognize immediately that in order to keep those promises, they'll need to put in the extra time at the end of the shift. There's no need for a supervisor to command, beg, or otherwise force the effort; members already know what is needed and why. This is the way, Steve told me, the operation has the best opportunity to meet its daily goals and commitments, and why the company enjoys one of the best records in the entire industry for meeting deadlines and getting shipments to customers on time. Every member is an integral part of the equation.

Apparently such methods are being adopted nationwide. In an "Inside Business" section in *Time* (1/12/04), the trend is described like this:

> The manufacturers that are succeeding aren't the type that build Company towns. They are too busy churning out innovative products. They aren't the ones blaming their troubles on unions—they're working with them to make their plants run better. And they aren't clamoring for protection from cheap imports either. They're competing furiously against them. They may never rise to the stature of yesterday's industrial giants, but they are redefining what it means to be "Made in America."

Months after my plant visit, Harold gave me a "Made in America" Plymold catalogue. It's a colorful, 185-page tabbed index book with every kind of restaurant seating and tabletop in every color and style you could ever imagine. As we paged through the catalogue together, he showed me the custom inlays one could obtain in the laminate tabletops: golf clubs, tennis racquets—you could probably ask for and obtain your spouse's or your cocker spaniel's profile imbedded in a table top if you wanted. The pages revealed an amazing array of cabinetry, millwork, decoratives, fine upholstery, both wood and metal chairs, and photographs of stunningly appointed restaurants with the Foldcraft touch. I was astounded at the breadth of products available from this company out in the cornfields.

Harold said that *all* products are made to order. The company doesn't keep much inventory of any finished product. There are, he said, over 2 million customer options available among the choices for paint, upholstery fabrics, laminate and color choices, custom tabletop edging and furniture styles. His soft voice seemed gently to question the need of the American consumer for this much diversity.

A customer picks out what is wanted and then the teams go to work designing, building, shipping and, in many cases, installing it. That's why those white boards at every team station are so important: to keep every cell responding to the real-time need and keeping deliveries on time. After all, those are promises to be kept.

If all of this sounds demanding of the members of Foldcraft—well, it is—but in a very positive way. Members here are learning the realities of running a business, understanding the critical factors for the success of their company, sharing the burden of care for their customers, "knowing the numbers" in their business that reflect excellent or substandard performances. No longer the sole domain of managers and single-owners, the truth about what the business is doing is taught to all of the owners. That's a demand still not often seen in U.S. businesses today. (More of this later in the ESOP chapter.)

The monetary rewards that we all seek from our work are inextricably tied up in those numbers, in the truth of a company's performance. At Foldcraft and in places like it, employees have a clear understanding of what they must do to make the company they themselves own profitable, and therefore justify bonuses and the high value of the stock they own. It's a cause-and-effect equation, and Foldcraft has invited everyone to participate in its solution.

The company's concern for its people and its social responsibilities extend also to its ecological and environmental processes. For example, Foldcraft burns its combustible wood shavings, scraps and sawdust in its boiler system to heat the entire plant for each winter season. This is accomplished in a steam boiler that features "scrubbers" that remove the particulates, thus minimizing its effects on air quality. Burning scrap also reduces landfill volume and the use of non-renewable fossil fuels. In our newly green times, such practices may not seem unusual or progressive, but Foldcraft has been practicing this form of stewardship for over thirty years.

There's another form of stewardship for which Foldcraft has become well-known. This small company has long been a leader in corporate charitable giving. While the average U.S. corporation gives 1.6% of its earnings to charity, certain groups recognize those who do better. Among the couple dozen companies nominated by the Council on Economic Priorities (CEP) in 1990 for their annual Corporate Conscience Award were some of the nation's giants: AT&T, General Mills, American Express, Xerox, Reebok, and PepsiCo. Also nominated was the not-so-giant Foldcraft. Here's what CEP's February 1990 research report said about Foldcraft:

> This small Minnesota furniture manufacturer donates 10 percent of total pretax earnings to charity. Its Corporate Mission Statement is [to take] 'a responsible and positive role within the community and progress toward a just, global society.' It emphasizes helping children in Third World countries and supporting groups that promote global understanding. Foldcraft employees volunteer time to a Company-sponsored clothing depot in which donated clothing is sorted and sent to needy people overseas. CEO Harold Nielsen, nearing retirement, has been selling stock in the privately-owned firm to its nearly 300 employees. Seventy-five percent now claim some ownership in the Company.

Ironically, that stewardship modeling was not always well received, even within corporate philanthropic circles. For several years Foldcraft Co. tried to convince the organizers of Minnesota's highly regarded Keystone Awards Program to include a 10% of pretax profit giving level, to be added to the 2% and 5% giving levels, at which participating companies are recognized publicly. The idea never gained support, so Foldcraft was told, because too many large companies could not give 10% and refused to be seen as second-level givers. The little company on the prairie once again tried to raise awareness and generate a little uncomfortable conversation.

Foldcraft's stewardship and stakeholder well-being is captured in an acronym Steve Sheppard spotted. Speaking to audiences about the company's early health and wellness initiatives, Steve would list six sources of well-being: Intellectual, Social, Emotional, Spiritual, Occupational and Physical. Searching for a way to remember these in order, he noticed the first letters spelled IS ESOP. For Foldcraft and its constituents, wellness IS ESOP and the magic in that phrase is the subject of the next chapter.

"I WANTED
TO WORK AT
FOLDCRAFT.
I HAD HEARD
THAT
MANAGEMENT
TREATED
WORKERS
WITH A LOT
OF RESPECT."

5

EMPLOYEE STOCK OWNERSHIP PLAN

Competing with some very remarkable and successful ESOP companies of The ESOP Association, the leading national trade group of employee-owned firms, Foldcraft was selected in 1998 as the Country's Outstanding Employee-Owned Company. "Quite an honor for a company in the cornfields," says then-CEO Steve Sheppard.

Having noted this achievement, I was also informed that in a similar ESOP Association recognition and award in 1993, Foldcraft's Shirley Bauer was named the Country's Outstanding Employee Owner. And I wondered what exactly had been happening in Kenyon, Minnesota, to warrant such accolades.

Before I started this project I had never even heard of an ESOP. If pressed, I would have quickly reverted to my literary background and come up with something vague about Aesop, the mythical 6th-century B.C. Greek slave who collected and shaped into fables many tales about talking animals. He's famous for stories that gave us such phrases as "sour grapes," or "crying wolf," "counting your chickens," and moral lessons like "The Tortoise and the Hare," and "The Mouse and the Elephant."

It wouldn't be hard to apply any of these plots or phrases to episodes in the lives of Harold, Louise, and Foldcraft, but an ESOP is a horse of a different flavor.

Many of you reading this won't need my simplistic explanation of an ESOP, but for preachers and teachers like me—and for many of the rest of the salaried workforce—a bit of definition is in order.

ESOP, as you have seen, is an acronym. The letters stand for Employee Stock Ownership Plan. It's a way for a business owner to sell a company—or part of it—and for its employees to buy a company—or part of it. Of the approximately 2 million corporations in the U.S. at any given time, about 14,000 are ESOPs. Not all of them, however, are 100% employee owned.

Why, we the uninitiated ask ourselves, would an employer/owner choose to sell his/her company to employees rather than to another entrepreneur? There could be many reasons:

1. To cut back on work but keep primary or partial control;
2. To recover some invested capital;
3. To protect his/her interests or dreams;
4. To protect the employees, the town, or the neighborhood;
5. To avoid hostile takeover;
6. To allow a tax-advantaged stock sale;
7. To enhance employee retirement;
8. To motivate employees;
9. On and on … .

In a 1985 speech, Harold Nielsen addressed all employees and their significant others at an all-company dinner. He alluded to the ESOP that was about to become effective on December 30, 1985. Harold admitted, he said, to "the realization … that I might not live forever [this from a man whose mother lived to age 104], and wouldn't need the Company where I was going."

He went on to say to his employees that he had mused hard and long about:

"....how best to dispose of the credits bestowed on me by our *corrupted capitalist system of which I had unknowingly become a part* ... . I devoted the bulk of my career to succeeding within that system, and now, I find myself disenchanted with the system—the same system in which the Company has succeeded. So now I sell a portion of it to you, who, in turn, become capitalists yourselves, wanting likewise to succeed within that same system. Hopefully, a long time before most of you reach my age, 69, you'll have come to some of the same awareness that I gradually have come to in the last 10 years. Maybe not. There is some kind of irony in all of that."

The original agreement transferred 49% of the stock to the ESOP Trust, to be redeemed by contributions to the Plan from annual Company earnings. In that agreement was a right of first refusal for the remaining 51% of the stock. In other words, Harold and Louise agreed not to sell the remainder of the Company to anyone else but the employees unless they refused to buy it.

Of course, no individual employee could stop this transaction from happening, even if he/she disagreed with it. It happened, as Harold put it, "without their consent," but was offset with the blessed awareness, as he also put it, that it cost the employee nothing.

The ESOP was, in effect, a profit sharing plan that resulted in gradual ownership by the members, the plant remaining in town, a recognition of the loyalty and efforts put into the growth of the company by its members, and the chance for those people to experience the capitalist system that Harold had come to know during his own years of ownership. Every new member of the Company would come to participate automatically after one year of employment.

This has got to be one of the intrinsic advantages of an ESOP. Steve Sheppard describes some others that hadn't occurred to me:

> Expectations of members are different when they are co-owners. Our relationship to just about anything is different when we see ourselves as owners of it. The relationships between one another in an ESOP company are changed, as well, since members truly begin to recognize that we are relying on one another's efforts in very real, tangible ways. These realities in turn tend to give rise to a greater corporate introspection, a more serious consideration of who and what the company is, what it stands for, what its legacy might be. This introspection often causes a wider focus on employees, since they are the beneficial owners of the firm. And this potentially dramatic ownership opportunity for wealth-building frequently generates greater engagement, teaching, and inclusion within the organization. The potential for all of these shifts are inherent in the ESOP.

I began to wonder how much workers are motivated by all this—especially since most of the benefits don't show up until later—maybe not until retirement, or until an employee leaves the Company. There is something to be said, however, for the idea that the better they work, the more they earn.

In a company like Foldcraft, everyone—or almost everyone—has to buy into the idea. Employees in a successful ESOP company, however, have a tremendous advantage over workers in comparable, non-employee-owned firms. Their ongoing working investment in the company results in ownership.

> An employee making $20,000 a year in a typical ESOP accumulates $31,000 in stock over 10 years, according to a 1990 study by The National Center for Employee Ownership (NCEO). That's no small feat considering that the median financial wealth was just $11,700 during this period. A Massachusetts survey done in 2000 found that ESOP accounts [nationwide] average just under $40,000. (*YES!* A Journal of Positive Futures, Fall 2005, p. 28)

Steve Sheppard pointed out that ESOPs have their detractors, despite the inherent opportunities in such plans. Here are some of their counter arguments and how Steve responds:

> *There are no guarantees in ESOP ownership.*
> Of course not. What owner of *any* business has a guarantee of success? Any entrepreneur takes risks hoping for reward. An ESOP simply includes employees in this risk.

> *There is a need for cash planning as participants retire or terminate.*
> Repurchase requirements, as they are called, require careful study, projection and planning, just like almost every other aspect of the company's

operations. If an ESOP company doesn't antici-
pate retirements, for instance, it can find itself in
a cash crunch.

*The debt service on an ESOP loan can be difficult
during a period of business reversal.*
Like any other debt a company may have, repay-
ment becomes a lot more difficult when the
company isn't doing well.

*There have been some pretty high-profile ESOP
failures, like ENRON and United Airlines.*
The malfeasance at Enron had little to do with its
ESOP. Some who run businesses are corrupt. At
United, the ESOP was created to help remove or
defer some pretty deep management problems. An
ESOP isn't built to do that. There are thousands
of successful ESOPs that we don't read about.

*Some Treasury Department "experts" claim ESOPs
lack diversification.*
By law, ESOPs are required to allow for stock
diversification after a participant reaches a certain
age and years of service. ESOP companies usually
offer additional retirement plans such as 401(k)s.
ESOPs are *ownership* plans that include retirement
plans. They are bound to carry more risk.

Fortunately for Foldcraft members, when Harold Nielsen
first sold stock to the ESOP back in 1985, the company had no
debt, had over a million dollars in the bank and the company

was growing. Those circumstances provided just the right back-drop to begin teaching Foldcraft members about the reality of business ups and downs. Successful ownership is almost never linear—lows are as real as highs.

Foldcraft employees are invited to participate in transforming and improving the company. Its "Lean Methodology" Kaizen teams (the word Kaizen means continuous improvement in Japanese) can dramatically change and improve specific elements of Foldcraft operations. The company has created a marriage between its ESOP and these teams, which merge the motivation to succeed and the means by which to do it. In a global economy, this combination of the intellectual, social, emotional, spiritual, occupational and physical, IS ESOP, is often the pathway to business survival.

Here's what it says on one recent Plymold (Foldcraft) catalogue. This introduction, aimed of course at prospective customers, just about sums up employee ownership and what it means to product quality and customer importance:

> Welcome to Plymold. We are 100% employee-owned, proud to carry on the traditions of service and excellence established by our founder, Harold Nielsen. Customers who have grown with us are still dealing with the owners.

> Our Company is our legacy. And the only legacy that endures for 52 years is one that values each and every relationship—with customers, suppliers, and each other.

> In an age when products and services are too often viewed only as commodities, our

commitment to customer satisfaction is what makes us stand out from the rest.

Whether you're new to us or are an old friend, a large company or small, you can depend on Plymold.

Just as you can depend on Foldcraft, and Winds of Peace Foundation, and Third World Friends Thrift Store, and Harold and Louise, and Steve Sheppard, and the current generation of Foldcraft stewards, and just about everyone else connected with this extraordinary operation.

"THEY
WILL·GET
OUT·OF·IT
WHAT
THEY·PUT
INTO·IT.
THEY
ARE·THE
OWNERS."

Chuck Mayhew

6

WINDS OF PEACE FOUNDATION

To contribute to global peace by promoting economic, social and environmental just relations. Our approach supports local grassroots efforts principally in Nicaragua.

In the United States we support transformational education which raises awareness of global inter-dependencies and fosters the change required to achieve such relationships.

Incorporated in 1978 and having evolved in significant ways ever since, Winds of Peace Foundation (WPF) adopted the above Mission Statement to reflect its intentions to be a different kind of philanthropic entity. (Should we be surprised at this?) It notes two major regions of work and investment—Nicaragua and the U.S.—and alludes to four major areas of focus: change of heart, creating peace, work in developing countries, and social justice.

What *isn't* obvious in the Mission Statement is exactly how WPF goes about its work. This organization works with its Nicaraguan partners, building on how Harold and Louise chose to be personally involved in the lives of those with whom WPF worked. Just as their early trips and personal presence in Central

America fueled both their vision and motivation, so today WPF seeks to be *physically present* in its projects. Mark Lester, WPF's permanent Field Manager in Nicaragua, has been a resident there for the past 22 years. He knows the land, the culture, the language, the politics, and the people as well as anyone can. His presence allows WPF to learn first-hand of community groups or cooperatives which seem compatible with WPF principles.

The WPF cornerstone resonates with those old ESOP notions of holism, participation and ownership such as:

1. Sustainability
2. Participation of people in projects based on local analysis and plans
3. Social change
4. Accompaniment of oppressed people
5. Community-based and self-directed development
6. Transformational education and training
7. Relationships and partnerships in grantmaking
8. Accountability and responsibility

The unique blending of entrepreneurial thinking, local presence, community initiative, dignity through accountability, ownership attitudes and infusion of capital might create the very best opportunities for self-sufficiency that the poor of Nicaragua could hope for.

In addition to Mark Lester's full-time presence in the country, WPF CEO Steve Sheppard travels there three times a year, and the full seven-member Advisory Committee, which reviews and recommends funding for the various proposals, visits sites every other year. This hands-on supervision of funding and operation is expensive and labor-intensive, and necessarily limits WPF to working in the central one-third of the country. It does, however, allow WPF to reach groups in that area which may have no other access to such resources—and, it works.

The Wisconsin Coordinating Council on Nicaragua (WCCN) in Madison, Wisconsin, distributed its December 2007 newsletter with a reference to one of its newest partners, the Hand to Hand Cooperative in Waslala, Nicaragua. WCCN has selected Hand in Hand as a beneficiary of its NICA Fund, "providing credit, employment, and hope." Back in 2000, the newsletter states, Hand to Hand received one of its very first assists from a little organization in Minnesota called Winds of Peace. They have now "graduated" to other agencies based, in part, on their successes with WPF. Winds of Peace has been a similar starting point for many organizations within Nicaragua, and has touched many lives.

In the years from 1981 through 2006, the following total grant and microloan amounts, in round numbers, indicate the priorities that have evolved:

Change of Heart	$20,000
Creating Peace	$56,000
Social Justice	$674,000
Developing Countries	$6,000,000

From 1981 through 2006 WPF has given away or loaned, without collateral, in the second poorest nation in the hemisphere, almost seven million dollars. Can one man and one woman make an impact in the world? It would appear so.

As I study my way through the WPF Handbook, reading short biographies of Board members, noting dreams, goals, cautions, modes of proceeding and all the other documentation needed to operate and control a small, multi-million dollar foundation, I am struck by an historical anomaly. The Foundation, under its original name of Children's Haven, was established in 1978. Harold's epiphany, from outward appearances and his own analysis, didn't happen until 1981. There's a three-year interval here. Was Harold more of a philanthropist than even *he himself* realized back then? Was Louise behind this? These are questions that even Harold is hard-pressed to answer.

Bill Gates' father, when interviewed, said that, "A huge concentration of wealth in individual hands is not healthy." The focus of the article was on his opposition to the repeal of the estate tax.

The Estate Tax is a powerful incentive for the wealthy to put their money into foundations and other charities, because such contributions are fully deductible. The Minnesota Council of Nonprofits, which sponsored his talk in the Twin Cities, released research estimating that the repeal of the Estate Tax would cost charities about $9.6 billion a year nationally and about $196 million in Minnesota (Minneapolis *Star-Tribune,* 10/23/03, D8).

A corporation organized to do business has a bifocal purpose: to expand the business and make a profit. A foundation is by definition nonprofit. It also has goals, but they have to do with *using* money and *spending* money, not making it. That creates options.

In the Cornerstones section of the WPF Handbook, Harold, Louise, and the Advisory Committee focus pretty carefully on who is going to receive their money:

> Those who are the neediest in the community should receive priority for assistance. WPF gives priority to projects that help rural communities, women, and indigenous people.

Listen to what the father's son, Bill Gates, the third richest man in the world, said to Bill Moyers on public TV (5/12/03). He started by relating his experience in Johannesburg, where he observed, *"Five miles out of this very modern city* is the worst poverty on the planet."

Gates the younger went on to say:

> "Wealth is a tool. Philanthropists can take risks that politicians can't. They can fund research, for instance, that has only a one-third chance of succeeding. A politician has to answer to his constituency for the two-thirds failure rate."

Rip Rapson, president of Minnesota's McKnight Foundation (which distributes $80–90 million/year) says the same thing.

Foundations, he said, take on "almost the role of social venture capitalists," taking risks, convening strategists, trying different models, "to get underneath the symptoms of social ills and work at the level of root causes." (Minneapolis *Star-Tribune,* 12/22/02, D7)

Taking risks against a possible failure rate is part of the strategy WPF uses in making Program Related Investments. WPF makes direct loans, guarantees loans made by others, and makes grants. These are mostly low interest, high risk, short term—and all without collateral.

Even Nike, with many millions of dollars more in resources than WPF, is also getting into microcredit loans, often $50 or so, in the Middle East—sewing co-ops, bicycle vendors, phone centers. It has (big deal—but don't knock anybody's venture into good works) loaned more than $2 million in Thailand, Indonesia, and Vietnam. (*Time,* 2/23/04, A5)

"These first time borrowers," according to the WPF handbook, "are among the poorest of the world's people. They usually have no collateral, and are mostly women and small farmers" … When they can't get such foundation loans, "They are forced to go to loan sharks and pay up to 10% interest *per day.*"

Some of WPF's loans are formulated through other agencies or foundations like the funding that goes to and then through NITLAPAN at the University of Central America in Nicaragua, and on to small farmers and businesses.

Foundations are regulated by the IRS. They must pursue their own stated goals and cannot be designed to create income for the foundation, to influence legislation, or to support candidates.

Remember when Scrooge was approached and asked to support the poor? Remember how he harked the solicitors back to public agencies such as poorhouses and debtor's prisons? Bill King, President of the Minnesota Council on Foundations says:

Foundations were never designed to fill the gaps left by government funding. Just as government has its distinct and appropriate role in society, so do foundations. Most foundations are created to last in perpetuity, so that their charitable resources are available, not just for today, but for future generations—to help ensure that there will always be financial support for the essential elements of a vibrant society. (op cit)

The affluent world always comes up with Scrooge-like excuses that make ignoring poverty easier: "Let them help themselves." … "They have too many children." … "They don't want to work."

Here's what Bill Gates, whose philanthropy focuses on health care, said:

> "Once you get health right, the Malthusian formulae are proven wrong—especially among women. Literacy rates improve, birth rates go down [We don't need to have so many babies if most or all of them survive.] And everything else improves."

Of course things can't improve much, even when funded by Bill Gates or the H & L Nielsens of the world, if the political and military climate in a target country profits by and thus perpetuates poverty and subservience.

That's what got the Nielsens' involved in School of the Americas (SOA) Watch. Harold, early on, joined Veterans for Peace, and in his interaction with and financial support of that group, he met Father Roy Bourgeois, a priest of the Maryknoll Order.

Burgeois, back when they first met, had just completed a six-year block of interactive peace advocacy work in Latin America.

Back in the states, from 1990 to the present, Father Roy has been an active opponent of the School of the Americas (SOA), partly as a result of the death of El Salvador's then bishop, Oscar Romero, who, Bourgeois said, was assassinated by graduates of the SOA.

SOA, in its 60 years of existence, has trained and graduated over 60,000 soldiers to go home and maintain by force, coercion, and intimidation, the status quo in Central America and other countries.

On February 21, 2003, I had a long conversation with Father Roy about the Nielsens and their support of his work. He knew I was taking copious notes so he spoke very slowly.

Father Roy is head of the School of the Americas Watch, which started modestly in 1990 with the goal of shutting down the SOA by educating congress and the American public about the links that connect SOA violence in Latin America with U.S. foreign policy and our international business community.

SOA began in 1946 in Panama. In 1984 it was forced to move to Ft. Benning, Georgia, by terms of the Panama Canal treaty. SOA was "closed" by Congress in 2000, thanks to Roy's protestors, whose number swelled from 10 to 10,000 by 1996. Unfortunately, it was reopened a month later, relatively unchanged, but under a new name: Western Hemisphere Institute for Security Cooperation (WHINSEC). By November of 2006, protestors at Fort Benning numbered 22,000.

So much for Congress's power to control the executive branch or the military.

Father Roy spoke in mid-March, 2003, to students at St. Olaf College, in Northfield, Minnesota, and outlined most of his and SOA Watch's involvement in U.S.-Latin American policy.

The Nielsens' support was mainly to provide public and media access to this issue. When Major Joseph Blair, a former SOA instructor, joined Father Roy's movement, SOA Watch used his testimony to produce an informative and revealing documentary video. The Nielsens and WPF provided most of the funding for its creation and helped distribute 8,700 copies to members of congress, college students, faith communities, peace movements, and veterans groups. Father Roy concluded our phone conversation by saying:

> "Harold and Louise have been not only friends, but have inspired many who are a part of the SOA Watch movement. They give us hope in these very challenging times in the struggle for peace and justice in the world."

Winds of Peace continues to evolve with the spirit and attitudes of Harold and Louise firmly in place. While the Nielsens have taken a less active daily role in the administration of the Foundation, their visions, hopes, outrages, sensitivities and mercies are manifest in the ongoing policies and practices of WPF. As Steve Sheppard observes, "What we are trying to sustain is the spirit and intent that Harold and Louise brought to the Foundation. The rest of us are simply stewards of those legacies, doing our best to care for the dream and learn from our partners."

7

CENTRAL AMERICA

Because we lived in Texas for four years, my wife, Judy, and I had visited Mexico, but we had our first real taste of Central American culture when our Minnesota hometown, Northfield, arranged a sister-city relationship with San Rafael, a San Jose suburb, in the Heredia Province of Costa Rica.

In the summer of 1993, someone from Northfield City Hall called and asked if we could house a visiting Costa Rican for a week. "Sure," we said, never dreaming how deeply our lives would be affected. That's how we met Alexander, ca. 30, who, on about the third day, came to calling us Mother and Father. We became well acquainted with the rest of the delegation also.

We were among a group of Northfielders who then traveled to Costa Rica in 1994. A year later, the wives of two of the original 1993 delegates came back and stayed with us in our home.

The coincidence (they multiply) in this, our introduction to Central America, was that back in 1991, when the Council on Economic Priorities gave its Corporate Conscience Awards, the only two Minnesota recipients were the H.B. Fuller Company in St. Paul and Foldcraft in Kenyon. We went to Central America with both of them.

Tony Anderson, a son of the late Elmer Anderson, a former Minnesota governor, was both CEO of H.B. Fuller and an ambassador to Costa Rica. Anderson and Fuller helped sponsor the Northfield-San Rafael exchange and entertained our delegation graciously on both ends of the trip.

Our journey to Nicaragua and Honduras in 2002 was the intitiation ceremony for, the handshake agreement to, and the study tour for this writing project. It was designed to do and profoundly did what was intended—to show Judy and me what the Winds of Peace Foundation was doing there.

We traveled, once we got there, with a group of about ten young men and women who represented American Foundations, some of them much larger than WPF—like The Ford Foundation, Public Welfare Foundation, The Global Green Grants Fund and Grass Roots International. The group was called Grantmakers without Borders. The tour was organized by Augsburg College's Center for Global Education and put us under the guidance and tutelage of Mark Lester, a former Maryknoll Priest, now the on-site director of Center for Global Education in Managua. He was our navigator, lecturer, interpreter, and our screener of safe and not-quite-so-safe edibles.

First some background. Here's what the Grantmakers group says about itself, and about its relationship to the Winds of Peace Foundation:

> Grantmakers Without Borders, a national network of grantmakers, works toward a just world by increasing strategic and compassionate funding for international societal change. Gw/oB exists as a moral imperative to expand strategic philanthropy and preservation of society. Winds of Peace dedicates foundation resources to work on this project.

The Center for Global Education, its offices housed on the campus of Augsburg College in Minneapolis, is also significantly funded by WPF. Their mutual interaction provides leadership and direction to Cross Boundaries, a program for tourists and employees, not only from Foldcraft, but for the curious like Judy and me.

In its Fall 2003 newsletter, *Global News and Notes,* The Center for Global Education included this short tribute for the information of its friends and supporters:

> Through the Center for Global Education's contract with Winds of Peace Foundation, the Nicaragua staff helped distribute over a quarter of a million dollars in projects in Nicaragua, focusing on leadership training for indigenous peoples, rural women's groups, and rural development in general.

That's what The Center and WPF, working together, hoped to be doing in Central America, and that's what Judy and I, traveling with young Grantmakers, hoped to observe. To indicate how it worked, I quote from a report, my *own* report, written for Grantmakers Without Borders shortly after our return:

> The tour went way beyond expectation. In just a week we visited over 20 urban and rural sites— offices, farms, classrooms, factories, co-ops, stores—mostly organized and operated by women. We were astonished at the industry, integrity, drive, and effervescent hope of these female entrepreneurs and the men who supported and often protected them. They operated these

entities on long hours and miniscule budgets. As an educational experience, this trip was graduate level.

An added bonus was traveling with those 30 year olds, all from foundation offices, all bright, engaged, loveable kids less than half our age. I wanted to take them all home with me.

Our experience was similar to, and as focused and as meaningful as many of the "Cross Boundaries" trips taken by Foldcraft employees. In a printout (March 1997) from a rather esoteric sounding organization called World Council for Curriculum and Instruction, Larry Hufford of St. Mary's University, San Antonio, Texas, writes about Foldcraft, and especially its Cross Boundaries program. He concludes his essay with interviews. The employees he interviewed may not be exactly typical of *all* those who have taken these tours, but they do show how deeply some participants have been affected.

The first, a male Foldcraft employee simply called "Participant 1" in the article, says, "I went down there to see what I could do for those folks and I was the one who was put on a healing path." Here's how it happened:

We met this woman … in Mexico City. … She encountered a human rights worker documenting abuses … All her film and documents were confiscated by the military and government officials … Men in her village who resisted [fought] a fierce battle with many deaths. Men who had fought would … just sit afterward as though they were in a daze. … She didn't understand.

I said, "Senora, when you are in battle you are only trying to survive, to protect yourself and those around you. Innocent people and children are trapped. After the battle you go crazy in the head. You are shooting to kill."

She asked, "How do you know this?" I said, "I was in war. I've killed. I think I killed a little girl. I know it makes you crazy." …

I was emotionally drained. I had tears in my eyes. This woman came over and hugged me. All the members of the group hugged me. (p. 14)

Kari Larson, in an article in *Business Ethics* (March/April 1995, 37) also documents Participant 1's experience. Before his December 1993 trip, she writes, he'd chime in with his buddies, "wetbacks this, wetbacks that." Talking with cane workers and labor leaders in Mexico's Chiapas region changed that. "A lot of produce wouldn't be grown without our migrant workers," he said, "and I don't look down on them anymore."

Larson notes that Participant 1's continuing involvement also includes volunteering himself and his truck to transport from Rochester, Minnesota, to shipping points in Minneapolis, medical supplies collected by nuns for destinations in Mexico and Central America.

Non-employees have had similar experiences, and with long-term results, such as Gloria Karl, a nurse, who for 35 years worked at District One Hospital in Faribault, Minnesota. A frequent volunteer at the Third World Friends Store in Kenyon, she went to Nicaragua to see where the clothes from the store were going.

She saw that, to be sure, but at an airport on the way home, she got acquainted with medical exchange volunteers from Plymouth, Minnesota, a Minneapolis suburb, who were doing an ongoing hospital project in Jalapa, Nicaragua. She got connected with them, and went with them on short-term medical service tours for *the next eight years.* She still leads groups there every year.

She spoke to her congregation about the work and they offered support. Her enthusiasm encouraged nine other nurses and three doctors to make multiple trips to the area. "Cross Boundaries" thus has had a ripple effect.

In a recent letter Gloria said, "I often think of how much I would have missed in life if I had turned down the Cross Boundaries trip. I have learned from this to take advantage of opportunities when they come."

A woman, "Participant 2," learned some things about the complicity of the U.S. government. When they went to the U.S. Embassy in El Salvador to report the arrest of a U.S. citizen and member of a religious order by the El Salvador military, the embassy representative said, "All we know is what we read in the paper."

"Believe me," she said, "we became more responsible U.S. citizens that day. None of us blindly accept what our government tells us anymore."

To cap off the experience, she said, "When we got to Nicaragua, the U.S. Embassy had been contacted and refused even to meet with us."

Another woman, taking the trip as a way of lessening the grief over the recent death of her husband, met a man whose wife and family had been killed and he himself severely wounded by the Contra military. Her own grief paled some by comparison.

I get this feeling that Harold, when he hears about interactions like these, will note well the negative reference to "the Central American military," and will mutter, "SOA—

School of the Americas." We have trained them in violence and repression.

Steve Sheppard says of these Cross Boundaries trips taken by employees and volunteers:

> Send people off on trips like this and they grow. They may return and say, "I know I'll never get to do this again," but they are so thankful—and they will have changed. They have learned something about themselves, their nation, and the world. That can only help when you are asking those persons to be creative, to think as owners, to think as global citizens, to think as global business persons.

Our trip was in many ways similar to the kinds of experiences Foldcraft employees had in Central America. In one of our early site visits, for instance, just outside Managua, we walked in to a large warehouse factory that housed the Women's Sewing Cooperative. The women were all sitting around, unable to work because a machine was out of order.

About 20 minutes into our visit I was sitting at an industrial sewing machine, screwdriver in hand, trying to adjust a double needle to mate with two bobbins underneath. "I can fix a Volvo car," I told the manager, "maybe I can fix a sewing machine." After ten minutes of fiddling, I never did get it to work. They needed the machine for a huge contract order of T-shirts destined for Maggie's Clean Clothes. The whole crew was idled because of the breakdown. It was a Sunday afternoon and their repairman couldn't be located.

I got hold of two publications afterward that focused on this period in that co-op. The first, dated December 2002, and published by The Center for Development in Central America, focused on the pressures of meeting large North American deadline orders with temperamental, secondhand machines, and with workers who were still learning their trade. Here is part of the article:

> The Women's Sewing Cooperative, it says, completed their order for 30,000 shirts for Maggie's Clean Clothes—but not without difficulty. First the cloth got hung up in customs, then the width of the cloth didn't fit the patterns very well. Then not enough cloth. Then the second order of cloth didn't match the first. Machines shipped from the U.S. had parts missing. Machines broke and re-broke. People quit, messed up, got tired, got sick.
>
> The broken machines were the worst. Their mechanic, whom they later learned wasn't very competent, wouldn't work on Sundays, came in late on Monday, and when the manager told him to get to work he was *very* rude to her. She fired him on the spot. It took over a week to get new mechanics, two of them, but they were very good. The machines became reliable and production exploded.
>
> The 30-day Maggie's deadline order took a bit longer, but they finished—and made a profit.

An article in the *Managua Monitor* only a month later said that the Sewing Co-op, in order to get some new tax breaks and perks, applied for Nicaragua's first worker-owned free trade zone status. The article backs into the history of the co-op, and describes how the founding partners invested 640 hours each as their share of the co-op. "For two years we worked without earning a salary of any kind. We the members built the building with our own hands," said Rose Davila, the Co-op Administrator.

The shop has employed 123 people in all, of whom 21 have entered into the year-long process of becoming members. In 2002 they produced for export 50,000 organic and conventional cotton T-shirts, and over 20,000 organic camisoles. The clothing they have manufactured has been declared by people in the industry to be better quality than anything that could be made in the U.S.

8

BELARUS AND MEXICO

A former state of the Soviet Union, landlocked Belarus, about the size of Minnesota, shares its western borders with Poland, Lithuania, and Latvia, its northern border with Russia, and its southern border with Ukraine.

Its capital city, Minsk, which today is home to nearly a quarter of its 10 million population, was 95 percent destroyed in World War II. To make things worse, in 1986, when the Chernobyl nuclear plant exploded nearby, 70 percent of the fallout was carried by prevailing winds to Belarus.

Each year since 1998, nine 40-foot container trucks, averaging 13 tons each, left the Third World Friends Store in Kenyon. Two thirds of those containers have gone to Belarus—all clothing and shoes. The other third of them has gone to Nicaragua.

Third World Friends is one of a number of groups that participate in giving these devastated people a boost. The program is called, "From the Heart," a Winds of Peace affiliate. In addition to clothing from Kenyon, they receive dried food and medical supplies from other groups in the U.S. and Finland.

The distribution takes place in Minsk, although bulk sub-shipments go to several other towns and to groups that address special needs, like societies for the blind, deaf, and handicapped, veterans' groups and children's orphanages and hospitals.

The spark plugs of this effort are Janna and Brian Anderson. Brian grew up in Minneapolis, Janna in Russia. Brian got interested in Mission work while still in high school, taking mission trips with the youth of his congregation, Vision of Glory Lutheran Church of Plymouth, Minnesota.

After about 10 mission trips to Mexico, Central America, and Eastern Europe, Brian settled in Belarus in 1994. There he met Janna, a native of Minsk. They met through the Christian church at Minsk and were married in 1997. They have made Minsk their home and "From the Heart" their work.

Janna has attended the University there, studying Russian Language and Literature. Their work is organized through "From the Heart," a Belarusian humanitarian organization. Their support comes largely from International Ministerial Fellowship in Fridley, Minnesota. They receive no established salary but depend on donations from individuals and churches.

The group, in Belarus, is not church affiliated, but is Christian in its staffing and outlook. Its work is to help, not evangelize, although it works comfortably and easily with area churches, sharing faith with clients only when appropriate.

During a recent visit Brian and Janna made to support organizations in the U.S., they were asking friends to help them gather funds for a used truck, with which they could transport clothing and other supplies to outlying towns and agencies.

They also work with a pastor from Redwood Falls, Minnesota, helping him with annual conferences in Belarus, translating while he is there—and managing his ministry between visits.

Although "From the Heart" is not overtly Christian, it is an outreach, and must operate under the constraints of a 2003 law that bans group prayer and in-house churches in Belarus.

The law grew out of suspicion, anti-church propaganda, and a desire by the government to protect the Russian Orthodox religious establishment. Obviously it is difficult for authorities in Belarus—as it is anywhere—to distinguish among those who are truly helping, like "From the Heart," and those who tend to exploit or simply to proselytize without regard to national, cultural, and ecclesiastical issues.

As I explore these various areas of outreach by Winds of Peace, I am more and more impressed with the caliber of people working on the other end in Belarus, Mexico, and Central America.

This is especially true of Cheryl and Cesar Uribe in Mexico. They are managers, house parents, and the moving forces at Miracle Ranch. When WPF bought the 120 acre parcel of orchard land at Valle la Palmas in 1983, the idea was merely to start a children's home.

On 80 of those 120 acres, however, stood 2500 olive trees and 1500 almond trees that were, at least in the view of the previous owner, under-producing.

Harold and Louise were more interested in growing good kids than in growing olives and almonds. The orchards came as both a potential benefit, and a risk-laden added burden.

Miracle Ranch has been, from the outset, heavily supported by WPF. Its $390,000 cash flow over 12 years has not only supported work with the children, but has also made possible scores of micro-loans, mostly to women and small farmers. Miracle Ranch has no source of income and has needed financial support.

In the following paragraphs I am borrowing heavily from a talk given by Steve Sheppard in 1990.

Getting Miracle Ranch started presented legal and technical problems. This was to be a nonprofit children's home and orchard in Mexico for Mexican kids, operated under the direction of and funded primarily by an American foundation. Back then

Harold and Louise called the foundation "Children's Haven." They eventually solved all the international legal problems and launched the children's home. Its mission statement, in part is:

> … to provide for the care, nurture, and overall development of each child within a Christian home and family setting, to cultivate intellectual, physical, spiritual, social, and emotional well-being in each child as a unique and special entity, and to emphasize the qualities of human kindness, respect, and love as both the right and the gift of every human being.

Within a year of its founding, Joel Mugge, founder of the Center for Global Education, arranged for Harold and Louise to meet the Uribes and their young son, Jason, born with spina bifida. The Uribes later welcomed a daughter, Nicole. The Nielsen and Uribe visions for children were on the same track. It was a fortunate meeting for everyone—for the foundation, for the new managers, and for dozens of kids who would be loved, nurtured, educated, and guided in this unique orchard setting by this dedicated couple.

Everyone who visits there is impressed with the boys. It is all boys, by the way, and on any given day there may be 10 or 12 of them, ranging in age from 8 to 14 years. These boys are polite, interested, and helpful to one another. They are, of course, a manufactured family—brothers, in the best sense.

Most of them come from abject poverty, some come without birthdays, are often parentless, usually victims of neglect. At Miracle Ranch they are suddenly clothed, housed, well fed, cared for—and educated.

Education is not a huge priority in much of Mexico, but it is at Miracle Ranch. The boys are taught by the Uribes, of course, but also by volunteers—college students on mission quests and internships, teaching them the 3R's, arts, crafts, and social skills.

It's still an uphill struggle. Sometimes, as these boys mature and try to put their newly learned skills to work, there are obstacles.

Take Gerardo, for instance (Miracle Ranch Newsletter of August 2000), who dreamed of studying medicine. Wheelchair bound from the age of three, he took an entrance exam along with 3,000 others, vying for 300 positions in the freshman class at the University of Tijuana. He never heard anything—neither acceptance nor rejection.

The Miracle Ranch folks then helped him apply to a private college that had a good pre-med reputation. Queries and entreaties to a Mexican child protection agency resulted in some re-thinking by the university. Finally, though, they shelved his application. The Uribes went back to plan B, the private college—where admissions had closed for the semester. Gerardo's dream had to be postponed—at least for a semester.

Such things happen to American kids also, especially victims of poverty and neglect. Another door finally opened for Gerardo. He decided to change directions and graduated from a community college in June of 2007 with a degree in graphic design.

Meanwhile, back at the Ranch, disasters and setbacks have added challenges. In 1993 the place was flash-flooded— a 20-inch rain—and became uninhabitable for three months. The boys were crowded into a private home while volunteers cleaned out mud and repaired the access road. The boys' dorm had two feet of water and mud, the main road was out, and the Ranch's four-wheel-drive truck had been completely submerged. The orchards sustained damage as well.

There have been three other less damaging floods between 1991 and 1997. All facilities were vacated for a week on each occasion.

Some years later (2000), after working all the angles to get a 4x4 passenger vehicle, one was found in Montana. A Minnesota volunteer agreed to drive it down, and after only a few weeks of glorious use, it was stolen from a grocery store parking lot in mid afternoon. Insurance covered the loss (stolen vehicles are rarely recovered there), but the process had to start over.

In a September 2001 newsletter was an article about the olive trees. Olives were not in much demand that year and olive flies threatened the crop, but a good harvest resulted. Forty tons were picked, with another 60 left on the trees—but no sales potential existed.

The chemicals used to cure the olives after they are picked were deemed too expensive for a volatile year, so the Uribes considered selling the crop raw, right off the tree, hoping at least for a break-even year.

Such are the challenges. But hope never falters at Miracle Ranch. The miracles are the boys. In a land where tens of thousands of children need such help, a dozen boys are surrounded by love, are getting the best of care, and are given the best of starts by people who believe in them, can see their potential, and will help them live up to it.

9

FRIENDS OF THE THIRD WORLD— THE STORE

This little book has, for about ten different reasons, taken several years to put together. One of the fringe benefits of getting involved with the Nielsen clan and their several foundation projects is that now I am also involved. I have been elected/ appointed to the board of directors of the Third World Friends Store.

I am a thrift-store nut, an habitue. I have bought clothes, shoes, books, telephones, glassware, and dozens of other things at Kenyon's Third World Friends Store. The selection is more varied than one would think, the price is superbly right, and what I spend there goes to a very good cause. Although I had shopped there for years (our dentist is only a block away, so I'm there at least twice a year), I got a personal tour as part of the research for this book.

On a cold January morning, I arrived in Kenyon at 7:50 a.m., stopped at the meat market, then made, exactly on time, my 8 a.m. dental appointment. About 8:45 I drove a half-block down the street to the Third World Friends Store, tried the front door, then saw a sign that announced:

HOURS: 9–5 MON–SAT

I had scheduled an interview with manager Dee Callstrom but was too early. Just then I spotted Dee, key in hand, about to open the back door.

I followed her in, but before we could settle down for our interview, she had to arrange a fan to blow heat from the warm back room to the very chilly front store. The steam boiler had shut down during the night. It was back on, thanks to Harold, but the place hadn't warmed up yet.

The store was COLD—maybe 45 degrees. I learned, just then, that among his other talents, Harold Nielsen also had a boiler operator's license. The boss had already fixed the furnace.

Dee put on a pot of Cloudforest Fair Trade Coffee (which they also sell), and we sat down to talk, warming our hands on the cups. "Let's talk about you first," I said to her.

Playing 20 questions, I learned that she was a Minnesota native, born in Wayzata, had worked in a nursing home, then got her real estate license and sold property both in Kenyon and Northfield.

She left that to work at the Laura Baker School, an old Northfield landmark that takes care of mentally disabled young people and adults. There Dee Callstrom got hooked on service-oriented work.

In July 1999, she began managing the Third World Friends Store. Harold Nielsen himself helped train her in and spent many hours a day at the store in those first weeks and months. Dee and Patti Jacobson (who works half time) and Steve Schiller, "The Loadmaster" as Dee calls him, are the only paid staff.

There are 20–30 volunteers, many of them women, most of them older empty-nesters who have both time and a variety of useful skills. The volunteers work according to their own schedules. Most of them have a favorite day or two a week to show up. Some days there are a half-dozen or more workers. On rare occasions *no one* shows up. Some have specific duties—stocking, arranging women's clothing, say, or books, or glassware. A few are trained to run the cash register.

Thelma, who lives in the nearby Kenyon Nursing Home, arrives by bus several mornings a week. She is one of the few who know how to run the cash register. She didn't need to be trained. She had, for 15 years, worked the cash register at the Bergh Pharmacy, the previous occupant and owner of the same building. Thelma works from 9–12 every day she's there.

Everything in the store is donated. It comes through the back door in—by request—plastic bags. Sometimes the pile of bags rises to the ceiling and volumetrically would fill half a garage. Then the volunteers pitch in and begin sorting. "The bigger the pile," says Manager Dee, "the harder they work."

We walked back to the warm sorting area. Here the volunteers open the black plastic bags and sort—clothing for the store, clothing to ship, other stuff for the store, other stuff to ship, occasionally things to discard. A few items go into a pile for washing and ironing. "Don't write that!" Dee shouted. She wants everything to come in washed and ironed and ready to sell or ship.

Dee Callstrom retired in the spring of 2008 and the board advertised, interviewed, and hired a new manager, Mary Tranby.

Mary has an interesting and varied background. A central Minnesota farm girl, she learned to work early. Her mother was aghast to see her husband teaching Mary, age 5, to drive a Farmall Tractor.

Years later, after majoring in mathematics and music at the University of Minnesota, Duluth, she began as a sales representative, first for a computer software company, and then for a dental supply company.

A victim of abuse in her first marriage, she bought the family farmhouse with her wages and started a home for abused teenagers.

Selling dental supplies, she met Tom, a dentist. Not long into her second marriage, she and Tom were off on the first of many dental missions to Haiti.

Mary has been running the store for six months as I revise this section. The store has added new merchandise and business has boomed, partly because of her sales background, no doubt, but partly also due to our nationwide economic meltdown. Mary's often chanted store motto also helps, "New treasures every day."

Meanwhile, in the back room, volunteers continue, under new management, to attack the mountain of donations that arrive day after day. On benches at a convenient working height is a line of boxes labeled with felt pen: MEN'S COLD … WOMEN'S WARM … CHILDREN'S WARM … etc., meaning cold weather clothes and warm weather clothes. Cold weather clothes go to Belarus, warm to Nicaragua.

Other boxes are labeled: HOUSEHOLD … SCHOOL SUPPLIES … HOSPITAL … TOYS … etc. All the household goods go to Nicaragua—pots, pans, dishes, silverware.

After the triage, clothing and some household goods and gift items that are likely to be sold in the store are priced and stocked up front. There is a good deal of high quality stuff, some of it new and still labeled and tagged from the area retail stores that donated it. Several area stores regularly donate clothing and other items to get a tax write-off.

Mary has hired Kris Robertson, an additional part-time helper. Except for one full-time and three part-time salaries, all the money that people like me spend there, indeed, all earnings from the store, goes to defray shipping costs to destinations in Central America and Europe.

In the back room, when the labeled boxes are full, they are pushed back off the bench onto roller conveyors, then rolled to the end of the line and onto a scale. Every box has a code number and weight marked on it. This is recorded in a ledger. By keeping track of the boxes loaded into a container, these weights can be added up to determine, fairly closely, the weight of an entire shipment.

Full boxes are wheeled over and stacked near the rear loading dock. When the pile gets big enough, a 40-foot Hi-Cube Container arrives on a semi trailer, backs up to the dock, and a crew of volunteers, men and women from Foldcraft, shows up to load. Filling a truck with boxes takes about 60–90 minutes. The container is government inspected, sealed, and then shipped off to an east coast port of embarkation, then on to Belarus.

Shipments to Central America go to a small port in northern Honduras, then by truck to Managua, Nicaragua.

In Nicaragua, clothing distribution is handled by a Jesuit order. Nicaragua, along with Haiti, is often cited as being so poor as to be classed as a "fourth" or "fifth" world country.

For the past 12 years, Third World Friends Store has shipped nine or more of these containers per year—625 uniform cartons weighing 13–15 tons per container. In 2006, nine containers held 134 tons of clothing and household goods. Three went to Nicaragua and six to Belarus. The ratio of adult to children's clothing in these shipments often doesn't reflect the younger population in the destination countries. Women do a lot of alterations, to remodel adult clothing for children.

Third World's efficient operation didn't start out with 30 volunteers and 134 tons of stuff. Third World Friends began in 1983 by accepting clothing in a different, much smaller building. At first, all the clothing, after sorting, went to an Hispanic elementary school in Southern California, then later to a border town, Tecate, Mexico. Fearing competition from the donated clothes, Mexican clothing dealers sabotaged the early shipments by spreading rumors that they were full of AIDS.

Shipments to Nicaragua began in 1986. Two years later, when the Bergh drugstore on Kenyon's main street moved to a new location, Harold bought the building. Kenyon locals thought Harold was loco to add that much new space for such an adventure. As usual, Harold's vision and commitment proved his critics short sighted. After only a year they nearly doubled the footprint of the Bergh building by adding an addition at the rear, a space designed specifically for receiving, sorting, storing and shipping donations.

Work in the former Soviet Union began about 1994. All European shipments go to Belarus, but in earlier years goods went also to Ukraine, Uzbekistan, and Latvia. Transportation to these sites has been coordinated by the U.S. government. Each shipment is inspected by them, then sealed and sent off to its distribution center.

One of the curious—and obviously unused—pieces of equipment in the Kenyon back room is a huge hydraulically operated shrink-wrap baler, and behind it, an electrically operated forklift. The U.S. government early on *required* this mode of packing and shipping. The machine made plastic-wrapped clothing bales four feet square and four feet high. They weighed 400–700 pounds each.

They did it that way for a while, until Harold exploded. He called Washington and read them the riot act. "On the other end," he said, "they don't have fork lifts to handle these quarter-ton bundles. Furthermore," he added, "square pallets waste a lot of space in our container trucks."

Washington relented. Everything is now shipped in labeled cardboard boxes of uniform size that weigh 35–50 pounds each. They are easy to handle on both ends and waste no space in the container. Bureaucracy listened. Third World Friends enjoys an excellent relationship with government.

Because of U.S. government regulations under the emergency aid "From the Heart" program, only clothing can be sent to Belarus. Nicaragua gets clothing too, but also kitchen, house-hold, school, hospital, and sewing goods and supplies. By weight, the Central America shipments are about one-third clothing and two-thirds household goods and other items.

Judy and I keep a little Third World Friends' trifold brochure on our refrigerator door. On it is printed a mission statement, information about Cloudforest Coffee, and then donation guidelines—what they want and can use: clothing, household goods, bedding, toys, books, small appliances, and so on. There is also a 30-item list of needed school supplies.

In Nicaragua in 1993, government spending per pupil was $43. By 1998, spending per pupil was down to $9. Compare that with my town, Northfield, Minnesota, whose school budget this year is $30 million for 3,800 students or $7,895 per student per year. School supplies sent to Nicaragua are greatly appreciated.

The brochure also lists what they *can't* use and *don't* want—in some cases because of liability, things such as baby equipment, life jackets, and motorcycle helmets, but in most cases things which they can't sell or ship, or for which they have no volunteer help to hook up and test—such as computers.

The back page of the brochure has addresses and phone numbers—and an ongoing request for volunteer help.

When I'm sitting in our dining room eating with friends, raving about the Third World Friends Store, probably pointing at my $3 trousers or $2 shoes that came from there, I say, "Just a minute," and run off to Judy's office to make a couple photocopies of the brochure. Many of our Northfield friends and neighbors now donate regularly to the store. I invite them to load donated stuff into the back end of my Volvo wagon. When it gets full I buzz over to Kenyon.

The Third World Friends Store is one place where our American addiction to too much stuff finds an outlet. Our surpluses are Nicaragua's and Belarus' treasures—well, if not treasures, at least useful items.

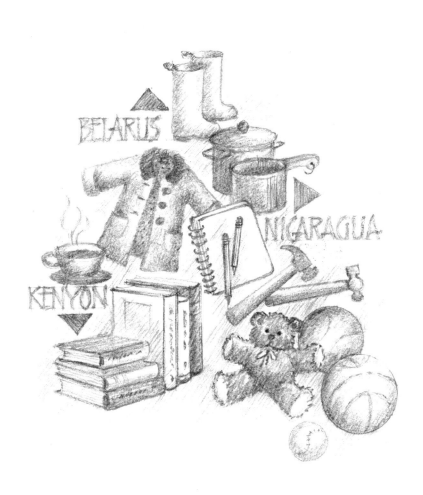

10

AFTERWORD

This little volume has taken a long time to write. The advantage of such procrastination, in addition to my joining the Board of the Third World Friends Store, and meeting and working with Mary, the store's new manager, is having gotten to know Harold and Louise far better over several years than I would have over several months.

I have spent some delightful hours drinking coffee and eating Louise's delicious baked goods in their Kenyon living room. We've talked about nearly every subject under the sun, exchanged books, shared contacts and friends, discussed politics. Louise has become our role model in demonstrating graciousness and good cheer. Harold has become like a graduate-level micro- and macro-economics professor.

I've had several tours of Harold's new pole-barn shop behind his house in Kenyon. It's big. There are a couple of antique boats and canoes in there, half restored, and the frame, engine, wings, and tail of an old airplane he says he and his nephew are going to restore. These are procrastinated projects of the sort I too cherish.

So much has changed over these many months. Judy and I have many good memories of the experiences and the wonderful people we met and traveled with in Central America and look forward to yet another visit in 2009. During these past months, the offices of Winds of Peace moved briefly from the Nielsen house in Kenyon to a small but impressive new office space in Minneapolis, and then back again.

In the big city, Winds of Peace shared that office building and often interacted with a group of other small non-profit foundations. During this time Christine Sartor was Executive Director of Winds of Peace. She resigned toward the end of 2005.

During her tenure, Christine worked hard at consolidating the foundation's benevolent focus and at interacting with other non-profits. She made a major contribution over several years as Winds of Peace evolved. Everyone I talked with spoke highly of her and appreciated her work.

A fortuitous concurrence happened coincidentally with Christine's resignation. Steve Sheppard got a big dose of the wanderlust at about the same time. He had been employed at Foldcraft for 31 years—he was CEO for the last 16 of them—and was getting restless. During those years he became deeply interested in the development of the Employees Stock Ownership Plan (ESOP) at Foldcraft and as a result became more knowledgeable and more involved in promoting ESOPs nationwide.

Richard E. Duffy, President of Ownership Visions, Inc., in Salem, New Hampshire, wrote this of Steve in January of 2006:

> Steve deeply believes in the core values of the employee ownership movement in America. He believes that employee ownership strengthens our free enterprise economy and of greater import, creates a broader and more charitable distribution of wealth while developing company cultures that maximize human potential by

enhancing the self-worth, dignity, and well-being of the person in the working world. Steve is committed to the belief that employee ownership can bring prosperity and economic justice to our free enterprise capitalist system.

In addition to his work with ESOPs, and partly growing out of it, Steve was leading seminars and speaking regionally and nationally about ethics in business. These were both his interludes and his joy.

For some time he had wondered if leading and encouraging were to be his newly evolving vocation.

Steve resigned at Foldcraft almost simultaneously with Christine's resignation from Winds of Peace. Harold put two and two together.

Steve Sheppard is now the Chief Executive Officer of Winds of Peace.

It was a natural move. Steve had been on the foundation board. He and Harold have been dear friends and on the same wavelength for over 30 years. A search committee was not necessary.

About this same time I was among those who nominated Steve for a Distinguished Service Award at his Alma Mater, Luther College, in Decorah, Iowa. Harold and several others wrote in support. Steve received that award in October 2006.

The award brochure mentioned Foldcraft, Winds of Peace, The Third World Friends Store, Miracle Ranch, the ESOP Association, and other connections and accomplishments. Judy and I drove down for the ceremony. It almost seemed as if Harold and Louise were with him on that stage.

If you have read this far, you will have shared something of the amazement that Judy and I have experienced in getting to know Harold and Louise Nielsen, and learning what they have done and will continue to do with the blessings showered upon them.

Harold was willing to let me write and publish their story only because reading it might encourage others to invest their funds, time, and energy into helping others.

"THE
ULTIMATE
TEST·OF
A·MORAL
SOCIETY
IS·THE·KIND
OF·WORLD·IT
LEAVES·TO
ITS·CHILDREN"

Dietrich Bonhoeffer

Steve Sheppard worked for the Foldcraft Company for 33 years, first as its Human Resources Director and later as Chief Executive Officer. He later became CEO of the Winds of Peace Foundation. Steve and his wife, Katie, now live in Decorah, Iowa. He is currently on the Board of Regents of Augsburg College, Minneapolis, Minnesota.

Steve Swanson is a retired Lutheran clergyman and college professor. He has written many books for adults and children and continues to write and preach as opportunities arise. He and his wife, Judy, live in Northfield, Minnesota.

Judy Swanson has designed and illustrated dozens of books and has created worship environments in auditoriums in many major cities nationwide. For 18 years she has designed the programs, backdrops, and sets for the annual St. Olaf College Christmas Festival.